The MAILBOX®
The Education Center®

Daily Math Prompts

D1472088

One math prompt for every day of the school year!

- **Review key math skills.**

- **Engage students in writing about math.**

- **Assess students' mathematical thinking.**

- **Prepare students for testing.**

Written by Ann Hefflin
Managing Editor: Hope Taylor Spencer

Editorial Team: Becky S. Andrews, Kimberley Bruck, Karen P. Shelton, Diane Badden, Thad H. McLaurin, Debra Liverman, Amy Payne, Karen A. Brudnak, Sarah Hamblet, Hope Rodgers, Dorothy C. McKinney

Production Team: Lisa K. Pitts, Pam Crane, Rebecca Saunders, Jennifer Tipton Cappoen, Chris Curry, Sarah Foreman, Theresa Lewis Goode, Clint Moore, Greg D. Rieves, Barry Slate, Donna K. Teal, Zane Williard, Tazmen Carlisle, Irene Harvley-Felder, Amy Kirtley-Hill, Kristy Parton, Cathy Edwards Simrell, Lynette Dickerson, Mark Rainey

www.themailbox.com

©2006 The Mailbox®
All rights reserved.
ISBN10 #1-56234-648-2 • ISBN13 #978-156234-648-5

Manufactured in the United States
10 9 8 7 6 5 4 3 2

Table of Contents

How to Use This Book

Select a Prompt

To support your math curriculum, the prompts are arranged sequentially from easier to harder skills. Begin with the first page of prompts and work your way to the last page, or use the skills grid on page 4 to help you choose prompts that best suit the needs of your students. The handy checklist on page 77 will help you keep track of the prompts you've used throughout the year.

Display the Prompt

Prompts can be displayed in many ways. Here are a few suggestions:

- Photocopy selected prompts and cut them into strips. Give one copy of a selected strip to each student or place the strips at a center.

- Make copies of a page of prompts and give one to each student at the beginning of the week.

- Copy the prompt onto the board or a piece of chart paper. Display the chart in the classroom or at a center.

- Make a transparency of the prompts to show on an overhead projector.

- If a visual is not needed, read the prompt aloud to students.

Additional Ways to Use This Book

- Use math prompts as
  - morning work
  - independent work
  - homework
  - a warm-up activity before beginning a math class
  - an activity for one math group to complete while waiting to meet with you

- Arrange students into pairs. Have each pair read and discuss the prompt before responding in writing. Or have the students in each pair complete the prompt independently and then discuss their written responses with each other.

- Take a quick assessment of your students' mathematical thinking by using the assessment rubric on page 78.

- Casually talk with individual students about their prompts to get a deeper insight into their mathematical thinking.

- Create individual student math journals by stapling a copy of the math journal cover (page 79) atop a supply of notebook paper. Or, if desired, use copies of the journal page (page 80) instead of notebook paper. Math journals are a great way to keep a running record of students' mathematical thinking and writing.

Skills Grid

Skill	Prompt #
NUMBER & OPERATIONS	
Number Sense	
comparing numbers	38, 56
creating and ordering numbers	36
comparing and ordering numbers	17
ordering larger numbers	172
odd and even numbers	22
place value	2, 23, 27, 28, 46
inequalities	41
expanded numbers	32
rounding	42, 73
Addition and Subtraction	
order property	53
addition	13, 31, 47, 57, 58, 61, 62, 63, 66, 71, 83
estimation	43, 73
subtraction	1, 7, 33, 72, 77, 81, 82
subtracting and comparing numbers	76, 78
addition and subtraction	12, 177
Money	
adding money	152
counting coins	141
coin combinations	136, 142
value of coin sets	6
counting money	51, 137, 143
subtracting money	151
adding and subtracting money	91, 148
problem solving	138, 147, 153
Multiplication	
basic multiplication facts	103
order property	92
multiplication	8, 87, 88, 93, 96, 97, 101, 107, 108
comparing products	106
multiplication and addition	111, 126, 178
multiplication and subtraction	146
Division	
division	16, 26, 113, 117, 118, 121, 122, 123, 127, 128, 131, 132
division and multiplication	98, 116, 133
division and subtraction	112, 169
Fractions	
parts of a whole	11
parts of a group	156, 163, 166
reading and writing fractions	157
comparing fractions (unlike denominators)	158, 161, 162
story problems	167, 168, 171
Problem Solving	
problem solving	3, 18, 37, 48, 67, 68, 86, 102
mental math	52
mathematical thinking	21

Skill	Prompt #
GEOMETRY	
angles	114, 125
plane figures	5, 15, 39, 64, 155, 164, 175
solid figures	44, 94
solid and plane figures	105
congruent figures	144
symmetry	29, 55
slides, flips, and turns	74, 134
problem solving	85
MEASUREMENT	
length (standard)	9, 25, 110, 119
length (metric)	14, 79
perimeter	154
area	159
perimeter and area	165
weight	145
capacity	130, 174
temperature	34
time to five minutes	45
elapsed time	90, 99, 176
calendar	60, 70
DATA ANALYSIS AND PROBABILITY	
graphing	59, 80
table	50
tally chart	19, 140
picture graph	35, 109
bar graph	10, 24, 120, 129
bar graph and tally chart	100
locating ordered pairs on a grid	180
certain, possible, impossible	65
probability	89, 150, 160, 170, 179
ALGEBRA	
shape patterns	4
number patterns	30, 69, 139
function table	54, 84, 104, 135
missing addend	49
missing subtrahend	75
missing factor	115
writing a number sentence	40, 95
problem solving	20, 124, 149

NUMBER & OPERATIONS

1. Bobby has 25 baseball cards. His friend Jack has 8 fewer cards than Bobby has. How many cards does Jack have? How do you know?

NUMBER & OPERATIONS

2. I am a 3-digit number. The digit in my hundreds place is 2 less than the digit in my tens place. The digit in my tens place is 1 more than the digit in my ones place. The digit in my ones place is 7. What number am I? Tell how you know.

___?___ ___?___ ___?___

NUMBER & OPERATIONS

3. Each student must have a partner for the field trip. There are 25 students in Class A, 26 students in Class B, and 28 students in Class C. Will each student have a classmate as a partner? Explain.

Class A	25
Class B	26
Class C	28

ALGEBRA

4. Copy the pattern. Then draw the next three symbols. Tell how you knew what to draw.

○ □ ○ ○ □ ○ ○

GEOMETRY

5. How are a square and a triangle alike? How are they different?

Answer Key

1. 17

2. 687

3. no; Explanation: In order for each student to have a partner, each class needs to have an even number of students. Class A has 25 students.

4. ○ □ ○ ○ □ ○ ○ □ ○ ○

5. Answers will vary.

6. Cole's piggy bank has 3 quarters, 7 dimes, 4 nickels, and 6 pennies in it. Cade's piggy bank has 2 quarters, 9 dimes, 8 nickels, and 4 pennies in it. Who has more money in his piggy bank? Explain.

7. Do you need to regroup to solve this subtraction problem? Explain your answer.

$$\begin{array}{r} 284 \\ -\ 168 \\ \hline \end{array}$$

8. Use pictures to solve the multiplication problem. Explain how you solved the problem.

3 x 4

9. Imagine that you work in a store that measures candy to the nearest inch. The candy is sold for a penny an inch. How much will this candy cane cost? Explain.

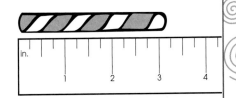

10. This bar graph shows Ms. Story's students' favorite colors. Ms. Story wants to get bookmarks for the class. The bookmarks are only available in yellow or blue. What color bookmarks should she get? How do you know?

Students' Favorite Color

	2	4	6	8	10	12
red						
yellow						
blue						

6. Cade

7. yes; Explanation: Regrouping is necessary because the 8 in the ones column is bigger than the 4 in the ones column.

8. Answers will vary.

9. 3¢

10. Ms. Story should buy blue bookmarks.

11. Write directions to tell someone how to find out what fraction of pie is left in the pan.

12. How does knowing your addition facts help you solve the following subtraction problem?

15 – 8 =

13. Write a story problem that is solved with this number sentence.

16 + 8 = 24

14. May and Donna were asked to measure this ribbon to the nearest centimeter. May says the ribbon is 7 cm long. Donna says it is 6 cm long. Who is correct? Explain.

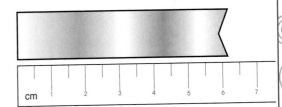

15. I am a four-sided figure whose sides are not all the same length. My top and bottom sides are the same length. My left and right sides are the same length too! Draw a picture of me. Explain how you know who I am.

11. Answers will vary.

12. Answers will vary.

13. Answers will vary.

14. Donna

15. Rectangle or parallelogram

16. Fred evenly divides 24 eggs into 4 baskets. How many eggs are in each basket? How do you know?

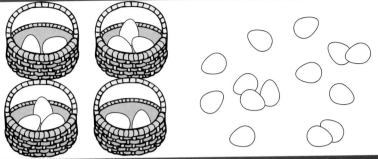

17. Write these numbers in order from greatest to least. How do you know the order is correct?

256, 318, 293, 265

18. Sue, Ben, and Jill are each writing a list of numbers from 1 through 50. Sue is counting by twos, Ben is counting by fives, and Jill is counting by tens. What are the five numbers that all three of them will write? Explain.

19. Amber has been rolling a die. She has written down each number that she rolls. Use her numbers to make a tally chart.

Rolls
2, 1, 2, 4, 6,
3, 6, 3, 5, 1,
4, 1, 5, 5, 5

20. Mike, James, Kate, Bill, and Jon are standing in line. Mike is second in line and Kate is third. Jon is behind Kate and in front of Bill. Who is first in line? How do you know?

Answer Key

16. 6

17. 318, 293, 265, 256

18. 10, 20, 30, 40, 50

19.

1	III
2	II
3	II
4	II
5	IIII
6	II

20. James

21. Read the problems. Write three more problems that have 10 as the answer. Tell how you decided what problems to write.

$$4 + 6 = 10$$
$$12 - 2 = 10$$
$$2 \times 5 = 10$$

22. What is the difference between odd and even numbers? Use pictures and words to explain your ideas.

23. Write the largest number possible using the digits 3, 8, 4, 1, and 5. Then write the smallest number possible. Explain how you found your numbers.

24. This bar graph shows the number of votes for class pet. Which pet has the most votes? Which has the fewest? How do you know?

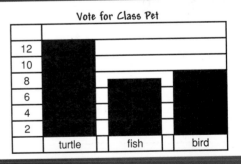

Vote for Class Pet

	12	10	8	6	4	2			
	turtle			fish			bird		

25. Sam wants to measure the floor and walls of his clubhouse. Should he measure in inches or feet? How do you know?

21. Answers will vary.

22. Answers will vary.

23. The largest number is 85,431, and the smallest number is 13,458.

24. The turtle has the most votes, and the fish has the fewest votes.

25. Feet

NUMBER & OPERATIONS

26. Eddie wants to plant 45 tulips. Each flowerpot holds 10 flowers. How many flowerpots will he need to plant all of his tulips? Draw a picture to explain your answer.

NUMBER & OPERATIONS

27. Write the value of the digit 9 in each of these numbers. Explain.

2,956

409

32,590

NUMBER & OPERATIONS

28. Matt is making a five-digit number. He uses the values on each card to make his number. What number does he make? How do you know?

GEOMETRY

29. Write your first name in capital letters. Which letters have at least one line of symmetry? Write to explain your answer.

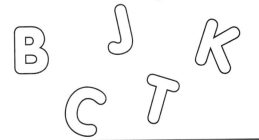

ALGEBRA

30. Find a rule for the pattern. How did you find the rule? Complete the pattern.

12, 13, 15, 18, 22, _____, _____, _____

26. 5

27. Nine hundreds, nine ones, nine tens

28. 17,645

29. Answers will vary.

30. Add, increasing by 1 each time. 27, 33, 40

NUMBER & OPERATIONS

31. Look at the grid. Find a pattern for each row and each column. Draw the grid and write the missing numbers. Tell how you found your answers.

7		9
17	18	
	28	29

NUMBER & OPERATIONS

32. Tommy wants to write 65,421 in expanded form. He writes 60,000 + 500 + 42 + 1. Is he correct? How do you know?

60,000 + 500 + 42 + 1?

NUMBER & OPERATIONS

33. Mark's team scores 6 more runs than Tim's team. Mark's team scores a total of 28 runs. How many runs did Tim's team score? How did you find your answer?

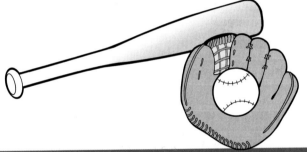

MEASUREMENT

34. Read the temperature on each thermometer. Read the season. Does the temperature make sense for each season? Explain.

Summer   Winter

DATA ANALYSIS & PROBABILITY

35. Study the picture graph. How many more grape snow cones were sold than cherry? How do you know?

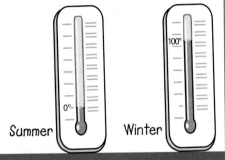

Favorite Snow Cone Flavors

Grape	🍧🍧🍧🍧🍧🍧
Lime	🍧🍧🍧
Cherry	🍧🍧🍧
Orange	🍧

🍧 = 2

31.

7	8	9
17	18	19
27	28	29

32. no

33. 22

34. no

35. 8

NUMBER & OPERATIONS

36. Write five different three-digit numbers using the digits 2, 3, 4, 5, and 8. Then explain how to order the numbers from least to greatest.

3   5   8
2   4

NUMBER & OPERATIONS

37. I am a four-digit even number. My first and last digits are the same. The digit in my tens place is 8. The sum of my ones digit and tens digit is 12. The sum of all four of my digits is 21. What am I? Explain how you know.

___ , ___ **8** ___

NUMBER & OPERATIONS

38. The school supply store sold 2,341 pencils and 2,431 erasers last year. Did they sell more pencils or more erasers last year? How do you know?

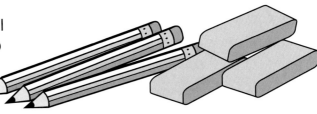

GEOMETRY

39. List the shapes used to make the robot. Draw your own robot using the same shapes.

ALGEBRA

40. Brandon picked a total of 30 apples. Fourteen of the apples were red. How many apples were not red? Write and solve a number sentence for this problem. Tell how you knew what to write.

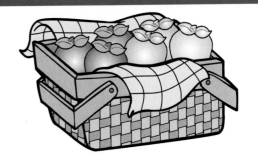

Answer Key

36. Answers will vary.

37. 4,584

38. erasers

39. squares, circles, triangles, ovals, rectangles

40. $30 - 14 = 16$

41. Use >, <, or = to rewrite each statement below. Explain how you knew which symbol to use.

391 is less than 421.
445 is more than 425.
201 is equal to 201.

42. Study the number line. What is the largest number that will round to 700? What is the smallest? How do you know?

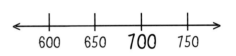

600   650   **700**   750

43. Copy the addition problem shown. Then explain how to estimate to find the answer.

$$490 + 245 = ?$$

44. Make a list of classroom objects that are shaped like rectangular prisms.

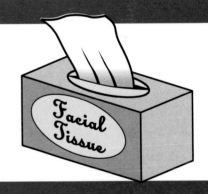

45. Read the time on the clock. Sophie says it is 25 minutes before three o'clock. Do you agree? Explain.

41.
391 < 421
445 > 425
201 = 201

42. 749, 650

43. Answers will vary.

44. Answers will vary.

45. No. Explanation: It is 3:25, or 25 minutes after three o'clock.

46. Make a list of all the one-, two-, and three-digit whole numbers that can be made using the digits 2, 4, and 6. Then write your list from least to greatest.

47. Draw a picture that models the sentence 24 + 35 = _?_. Solve the problem. Explain how the picture helped you solve the problem.

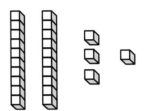

48. Ted sells boxes of chocolate chip cookies and boxes of sugar cookies. If he sells a total of 50 boxes of cookies, what are three possible combinations of chocolate chip and sugar cookie boxes sold? How do you know?

chocolate chip cookies

sugar cookies

49. If ♡ = 3 and ♡ + ☺ = 7, then what is the value of *x* in the problem shown?

$$\heartsuit + \heartsuit + \smiley + \smiley = x$$

50. Look at the table. Were more lunches sold altogether on Tuesday and Wednesday or on Wednesday and Thursday? Tell how you know.

Lunch Sales for the Week	
Day of the Week	Number of Lunches Sold
Monday	24
Tuesday	61
Wednesday	48
Thursday	55
Friday	72

46. 2, 4, 6, 24, 26, 42, 46, 62, 64, 246, 264, 426, 462, 624, 642

47. 59

48. Answers will vary.

49. $x = 14$

50. More lunches were sold on Tuesday and Wednesday.

51. Sid has 1 five-dollar bill, 3 one-dollar bills, 4 quarters, 6 dimes, 3 nickels, and 7 pennies. How much money does he have? Explain how you found your answer.

52. Read the problem. Try to solve the problem in your head. Tell why it is better to solve some math problems in your head.

12,000 + 10,000

53. Alex thinks that 14 + 6 = 6 + 14. Do you agree? Draw a picture to explain your answer.

54. Write the rule for this table. How do you know this is the rule?

In	2	3	4	5	6
Out	7	8	9	10	11

55. Copy the shapes. Draw lines of symmetry on each one. Remember that some shapes may have more than one line of symmetry.

51. $9.82

52. 22,000

53. Alex is correct.

54. Add 5.

55.

NUMBER & OPERATIONS

56. Tommy sold 37 T-shirts. Tina sold 52 T-shirts. Terry sold more T-shirts than Tommy, but fewer than Tina. Which is a possible number of T-shirts sold by Terry? How do you know?

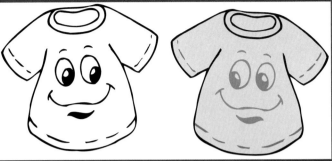

30 50 60 36

NUMBER & OPERATIONS

57. Copy and solve this addition problem. Write the steps that tell how to solve the problem.

375 + 255

NUMBER & OPERATIONS

58. Look at the magic square. Complete the square so that each row and column adds up to the same sum. Tell how you got your answers.

7		12
	10	
8		13

DATA ANALYSIS & PROBABILITY

59. Claire asks each of her classmates which day of the week is his or her favorite. What is the best way for Claire to display the answers? Tell why you think so.

Sunday
Monday
Tuesday
Wednesday
Thursday
Friday
Saturday

MEASUREMENT

60. Shelly has taken piano lessons for 59 days. Tom has taken lessons for 8 weeks. Frank has taken lessons for 6 weeks and 5 days. Who has taken lessons for the longest amount of time? Who has taken lessons for the shortest amount of time? How do you know?

Answer Key

56. 50

57. 630

58.

7	11	12
15	10	5
8	9	13

59. Answers will vary.

60. Shelly has taken lessons the longest amount of time. Frank has taken lessons the shortest amount of time.

61. James delivered 1,465 newspapers. Juan delivered 1,596 newspapers. How many newspapers did the boys deliver in all? How do you know?

62. Nancy is solving the problem. She starts by adding 6 + 7 + 2. Is she correct? How do you know? What is the correct answer to this problem?

$$356$$
$$78$$
$$+\ 402$$

63. Use the digits 1, 2, 3, 4, 5, and 6 to create an addition problem in the boxes shown. Solve the problem. Write a word problem using the addition problem you made.

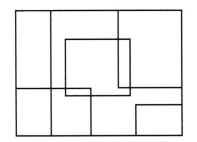

64. Find the total number of rectangles in this design. Then make a design of your own using at least five triangles.

65. Write the letters A, B, and C on your paper. Next to each letter, write whether each statement below is impossible, possible, or certain. How do you know?

A. One hour after 6:00 P.M. is 7:00 P.M.

B. You can jump from one end of a football field to the other end in one long jump.

C. You will drop your pencil on the floor.

61. 3,061

62. no, 836

63. Answers will vary.

64. 12

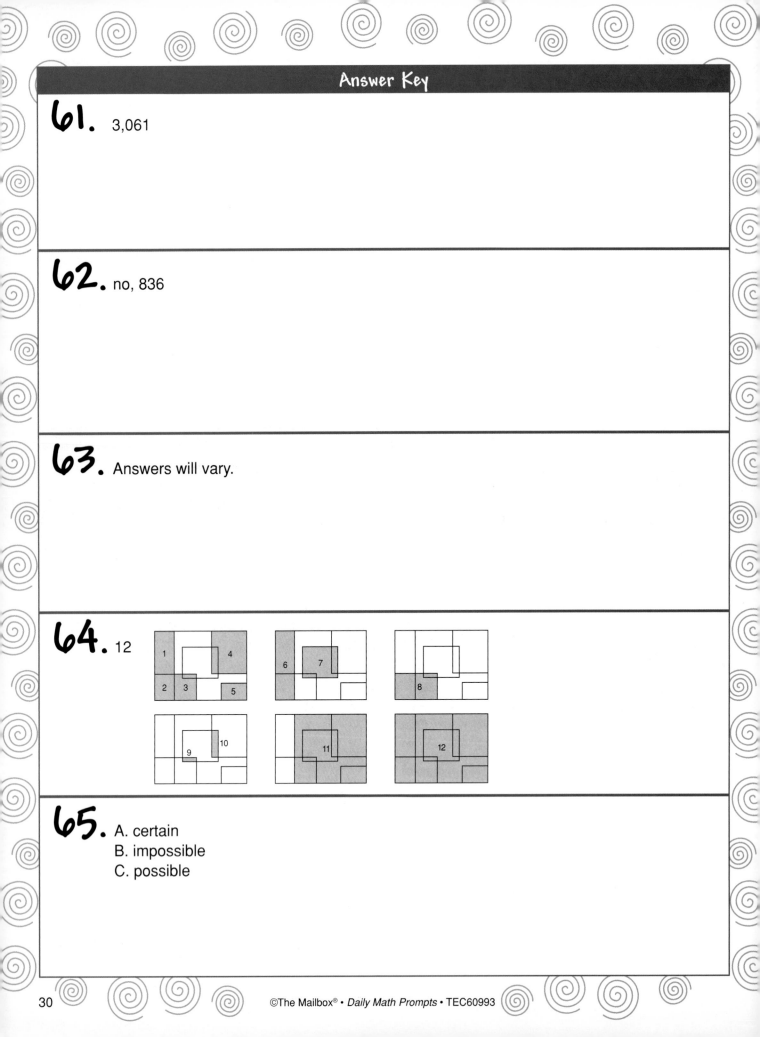

65. A. certain
B. impossible
C. possible

NUMBER & OPERATIONS

66. There are 86 third graders, 65 fourth graders, and 72 fifth graders. The principal ordered 225 Frisbee discs. Did he order enough for each child to have one? Explain.

NUMBER & OPERATIONS

67. Read the problem. Write a word problem that matches it. Then solve the word problem.

$$75 + 108 - 62$$

NUMBER & OPERATIONS

68. Stan and Eddie sell wrapping paper. They sold 200 rolls in one month. Stan sold 30 more rolls than Eddie. How many rolls did each boy sell? How do you know?

ALGEBRA

69. Jen made 12 bookmarks on Monday, 24 on Tuesday, and 36 on Wednesday. If this pattern continues, how many bookmarks will she have made in all by Saturday? Draw a picture or make a table to explain your answer.

MEASUREMENT

70. Matt has a test today. He has been studying for it for three weeks. Today is Thursday the 29th. On what day did Matt begin to study? How do you know?

S	M	T	W	Th	F	S
				1	2	3
4	5	6	7	8	9	10
11	12	13	14	15	16	17
18	19	20	21	22	23	24
25	26	27	28	29	30	

66. yes

67. Word problems will vary.   121

68. Stan sold 115 and Eddie sold 85.

69. 252

70. Thursday the 8th

S	M	T	W	Th	F	S
				1	2	3
4	5	6	7	8 START DAY	9	10
11	12	13	14	15	16	17
18	19	20	21	22	23	24
25	26	27	28	29 TEST DAY	30	

NUMBER & OPERATIONS

71. Six schools want to go on a field trip to a concert. The concert hall holds 275 people. There are three concert times. Arrange the six school groups so that everyone will be able to attend the concert.

| Wayside–142 students | Glen Oaks–160 students | Hillcrest–130 students |
| Saint Mary's–68 students | Jefferson–115 students | Washington–205 students |

NUMBER & OPERATIONS

72. There were 18 cupcakes on the table this morning. More cupcakes were added after lunch. Now there are 35 cupcakes. How many cupcakes were placed on the table after lunch? Explain your answer using pictures and words.

NUMBER & OPERATIONS

73. Read the subtraction problem. Estimate the answer to the nearest hundred. Write each step in words as you solve the problem.

$$335 - 210 =$$

GEOMETRY

74. Study the picture. Does the picture show a flip, a slide, or a turn? Explain the difference between a flip, a slide, and a turn.

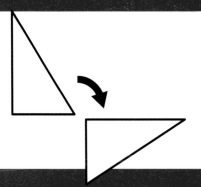

ALGEBRA

75. Find the missing number. How did you find the number?

$$25 - \underline{\quad\quad} = 12$$

71. Wayside and Hillcrest; Saint Mary's and Washington; Glen Oaks and Jefferson

72. 17

73. 300 – 200 = 100, 335 – 210 = 125

74. turn; You flip an object over a line. You turn an object around a central point. You slide an object to a new spot without flipping or turning it.

75. 13

NUMBER & OPERATIONS

76. Katie says that (867 − 53) < (952 − 103). Use estimation to find out whether she is correct. Explain your answer.

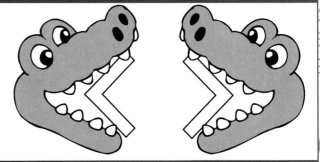

NUMBER & OPERATIONS

77. Dana collected 425 stamps. She wants to show 345 to her class. How many stamps does she want to leave at home? How do you know?

NUMBER & OPERATIONS

78. Clay started baking cookies on Tuesday. He baked a total of 365 cookies. On Wednesday he baked 145 cookies. On Thursday he baked 160 cookies. How many cookies did he bake on Tuesday? How do you know?

MEASUREMENT

79. Mike wants to measure the distance from his classroom to the cafeteria in millimeters. Then he wants to measure the thickness of a penny in centimeters. Finally, he wants to measure the length of his pencil in meters. Are these the best metric units of measure for him to use for each object? How do you know your answers are correct?

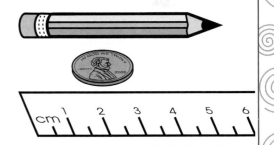

DATA ANALYSIS & PROBABILITY

80. Brandon asks his teammates what day they would like to practice. Their answers are Monday, Monday, Friday, Saturday, Saturday, Tuesday, Wednesday, Monday, Friday, Tuesday, Tuesday, Wednesday, and Tuesday. What is the best way for him to show this information? Explain your answer.

76. Yes, she is correct.

77. 80

78. 60

79. no; Explanation: He should measure the distance from his classroom to the cafeteria in meters, the thickness of a penny in millimeters, and the length of his pencil in centimeters.

80. Answers will vary.

81. The Ocean Sound Ferry can carry 375 people at one time. If 542 people buy tickets, how many people will have to wait for the next trip? How do you know?

82. Last year, students raised $3,375 for school supplies. This year, they raised $4,020. How much more money was raised this year than last year? How do you know?

83. Dora is thinking of two mystery numbers. The sum of the numbers is 138. One number is 32 more than the other. What are the two numbers? Explain how you solved this problem.

? + ? = 138

84. Create your own in-and-out table using the rule "multiply by 2." Explain how you decided what numbers to use.

In					
Out					

85. These are Dibbles.

These are not Dibbles.

Is this a Dibble?

Explain how you know.

81. 167

82. $645

83. 85 and 53

84. Answers will vary.

85. yes; Explanation: Dibbles are squares or rectangles with shapes inside.

NUMBER & OPERATIONS

86. Write one addition and one multiplication word problem to match the picture.

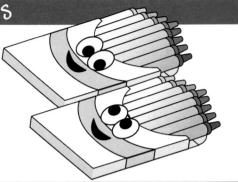

NUMBER & OPERATIONS

87. Jim's mom bought 5 boxes of granola bars. Each box contains 6 bars. How many granola bars did Jim's mom buy all together? Draw a picture to show your answer.

NUMBER & OPERATIONS

88. Pedro is solving this problem. How can he use a pattern to find the answer?

$$6 \times 4 = \underline{\ ?\ }$$

DATA ANALYSIS & PROBABILITY

89. Andy has 10 blue, 2 brown, 10 green, and 14 red socks. If he grabs a sock without looking, which color is most likely to be picked? Which color is least likely to be picked? Which colors are equally likely to be picked? Explain your answers.

MEASUREMENT

90. Based on the train schedule shown, does it take longer to get to Triangle City or Math Junction? How do you know?

Local Train Schedule		
To	Departs	Arrives
Triangle City	8:00 A.M.	1:00 P.M.
Numberville	9:00 A.M.	Noon
Math Junction	10:00 A.M.	2:00 P.M.

86. Answers will vary.

87. 30

88. Answers will vary. Explanation: Students may say that they could count by 4's or by 6's.

89. Red is most likely to be picked. Brown is least likely to be picked. Blue and green are equally likely to be picked.

90. Triangle City

NUMBER & OPERATIONS

91. Ollie has 1 five-dollar bill, 8 one-dollar bills, and 6 quarters. If he buys a game that costs $9.55, how much money will he have left? How do you know?

NUMBER & OPERATIONS

92. Sue says that 3 x 9 is the same as 9 x 3. Is she right? Use words and pictures to explain your answer.

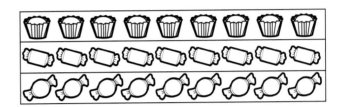

NUMBER & OPERATIONS

93. Taylor needs to add 8 buttons to each of 9 shirts. How many buttons will she need in all? Write a number sentence and draw a picture to show your answer.

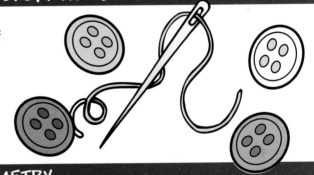

GEOMETRY

94. Emma says that a cube has the same number of faces as edges. Is she correct? How do you know?

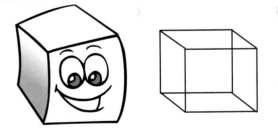

ALGEBRA

95. Toby has 6 equal groups of marbles. If he has 42 marbles altogether, how many marbles are in each group? Solve the problem by writing a number sentence.

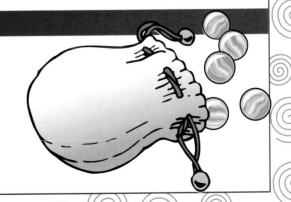

91. $4.95

92. yes

93. 72

94. no

95. 7

NUMBER & OPERATIONS

96. Replace one factor in each problem with zero. Then write and solve the new problems. What do you notice about all of the new products? Explain what happened.

$$4 \times 3 = 12 \qquad 6 \times 9 = 54$$
$$7 \times 4 = 28$$

NUMBER & OPERATIONS

97. Dillon sorts his bottle caps into 4 groups of 8. He says that he can find the total number of bottle caps by doubling 2 x 8. Is he right? Explain.

NUMBER & OPERATIONS

98. Write one multiplication fact and one division fact for the picture. Explain how you found your answer.

```
X X X X X
X X X X X
X X X X X
```

MEASUREMENT

99. Mark arrived at school at 8:15 A.M. He left school at 3:45 P.M. How long was Mark at school? Explain.

DATA ANALYSIS & PROBABILITY

100. After a field trip to the zoo, Mr. Lion's class completed the tally chart shown. Use this data to create a bar graph. How did you know what to draw?

Favorite Zoo Animals	
Animal	Tally Marks
Elephant	‖‖‖
Monkey	‖‖‖ ‖‖‖ ‖‖
Tiger	‖‖
Penguin	‖
Seal	‖‖‖ ‖

96. All of the products equal zero.

97. yes

98. Answers may vary.

99. 7 hours 30 minutes

100. Graphs may vary slightly.

Favorite Zoo Animals

NUMBER & OPERATIONS

101. Write a multiplication problem that has a product of 30. Then write a word problem to match it.

____?____ x ____?____ = 30

NUMBER & OPERATIONS

102. I am a two-digit number between 30 and 40. I am a multiple of 4, 6, and 9. What number am I? Tell how you know.

30   **?**   **40**

NUMBER & OPERATIONS

103. Multiples of 5 always end in either a 0 or a 5. What other hints or patterns do you know to help memorize the different multiplication facts from 0 to 10?

ALGEBRA

104. Seth says that the rule for the table shown is "multiply by 4." Is he right? Explain.

In	4	5	6	7	8
Out	16	20	24	28	32

GEOMETRY

105. How is a circle similar to a cylinder? How is it different?

101. Answers will vary.

102. 36

103. Answers will vary.

104. yes

105. Answers will vary.

NUMBER & OPERATIONS

106. Is the product of (8 x 6) x 5 less than, greater than, or equal to the product of (5 x 6) x 8? How do you know?

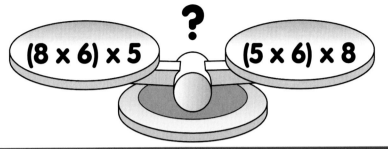

NUMBER & OPERATIONS

107. Tell two ways to solve the multiplication problem. Use one method to solve the problem, and then check your answer by using the other method.

14 x 5

NUMBER & OPERATIONS

108. Movie tickets cost $5. If the theater sells 68 tickets, how much money does it earn? What did you do to find out?

DATA ANALYSIS & PROBABILITY

109. Sally wants to make a picture graph to show her friends' favorite sandwiches. Look at the information and the key. How many symbols will she draw for each type of sandwich? Explain your answers.

ham and cheese = 11
peanut butter and jelly = 8
tuna = 2

Key
👤 = 2 friends

MEASUREMENT

110. Brady sells bracelets for 50¢ per half inch. How much will he charge for this bracelet? Explain your answer.

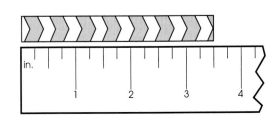

106. The products are the same.

107. 70

108. $340

109. ham and cheese: 5½ symbols; peanut butter and jelly = 4 symbols; tuna = 1 symbol

110. $3.50

NUMBER & OPERATIONS

111. Mary sold 3 times as many candy bars as Frances. Ella sold twice as many candy bars as Mary. Frances sold 8 candy bars. How many candy bars did the three girls sell in all? Explain your answers.

NUMBER & OPERATIONS

112. How are division and subtraction alike? How are they different?

NUMBER & OPERATIONS

113. The coach divides the soccer team into groups of 6. If there are 18 players, how many groups are there? How do you know your answer is correct?

GEOMETRY

114. The toy store prices its kites based on the information shown. How much does this kite cost? Explain your answer.

angles = 50¢ each

ALGEBRA

115. If △ = 3, find the value of □ and ○. How do you know?

$$\square \div \triangle = 12$$

$$\bigcirc \times 9 = \square$$

Answer Key

111. 80

112. Answers will vary.

113. 3

114. $8.00; Explanation: There are 16 angles.

115. □ = 36, ◯ = 4

116. Carly has 42 hair ribbons. She wants to hang them on 7 hangers. Does knowing that $6 \times 7 = 42$ help her decide how many hair ribbons to hang on each hanger? How?

117. Dan and Ray are playing a spinning game. Each time a player spins a whole number that can be divided evenly by both 3 and 4, that player gets a point. Which player has earned more points? How did you find out?

| Dan's spins | 12 | 20 | 28 | 46 | 60 |
| Ray's spins | 16 | 24 | 36 | 48 | 60 |

118. Fiona will be taking care of the class fish over the summer. If she keeps it for 63 days, how many weeks will she have it? Explain how you know.

119. Kim needs 3 yards of fabric and 5 feet of ribbon. The fabric store only sells fabric in feet and ribbon in inches. How many feet of fabric should she buy? How many inches of ribbon should she buy?

120. Babe's team played ten baseball games in April. Study the graph. Write two true statements about the graph. Tell how you know. Explain why each statement is true.

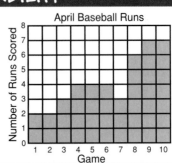

April Baseball Runs

116. Answers will vary.

117. Ray; Explanation: Dan has scored 2 points;
Ray has scored 4 points.

118. 9

119. 9 feet of fabric, 60 inches of ribbon

120. Answers will vary.

NUMBER & OPERATIONS

121. Fran's Fudge Shop is giving away boxes of candy. Yesterday Fran gave 56 boxes to 8 people. Those people divided the boxes equally. Today she gave 72 boxes to 9 people. Those people divided the boxes equally. On which day did each person get the most boxes of candy? How do you know?

NUMBER & OPERATIONS

122. Solve the problem. Then write and illustrate a story problem to go with it.

$$54 \div 9 =$$

NUMBER & OPERATIONS

123. Ninety-five students are going on a field trip. If the teacher needs one parent to lead each group of five students, how many parents does she need? How do you know?

ALGEBRA

124. Juan is packing 56 CDs in boxes. Each box holds 8 CDs. Which number sentence will help Juan decide how many boxes he needs to hold his CDs? How do you know? How many boxes will he need?

$$56 \times 8 = \square$$
$$56 \div 8 = \square$$

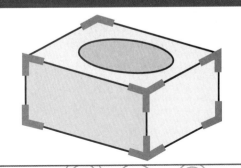

GEOMETRY

125. Make a list of objects that have right angles. Think of things that are in your classroom and things that are around your school. Choose several items and draw each one. Highlight the right angle(s) in each drawing.

121. today

122. 6

123. 19

124. $56 \div 8 = \Box$, 7

125. Answers will vary.

NUMBER & OPERATIONS

126. On Monday, Mom uses 8 teaspoons of sugar to make 2 quarts of tea. On Tuesday, she uses 12 teaspoons of sugar to make 3 quarts of tea. On Wednesday, she uses 16 teaspoons of sugar to make 4 quarts of tea. If the pattern continues, how many total quarts of tea will she have made by Friday? How many total teaspoons of sugar will she have used to make the tea? How do you know?

NUMBER & OPERATIONS

127. The tables in the cafeteria each seat 8 students. If there are 68 students in the cafeteria, what is the smallest number of tables needed? Explain your answer with words and pictures.

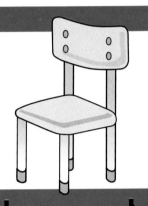

NUMBER & OPERATIONS

128. Ms. Scott put 60 choir students into 5 equal groups. She then divided each group into trios. If Ms. Scott needs a set of sheet music for each trio, how many sets of sheet music does she need for the choir in all? How do you know?

DATA ANALYSIS & PROBABILITY

129. Elsie surveyed her friends to find out how many glasses of milk they drink each day. Their answers were 1, 2, 0, 4, 2, 3, 3, 3, 0, and 1. Help Elsie display this information on a bar graph.

MEASUREMENT

130. How could you figure out whether these two containers hold the same amount of juice? How could you check your answer?

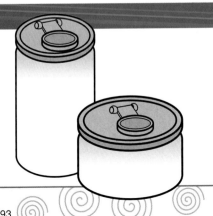

126. 20 quarts of tea, 80 teaspoons of sugar

127. 9

128. 20

129. Graphs will vary slightly.

How Many Glasses of Milk?

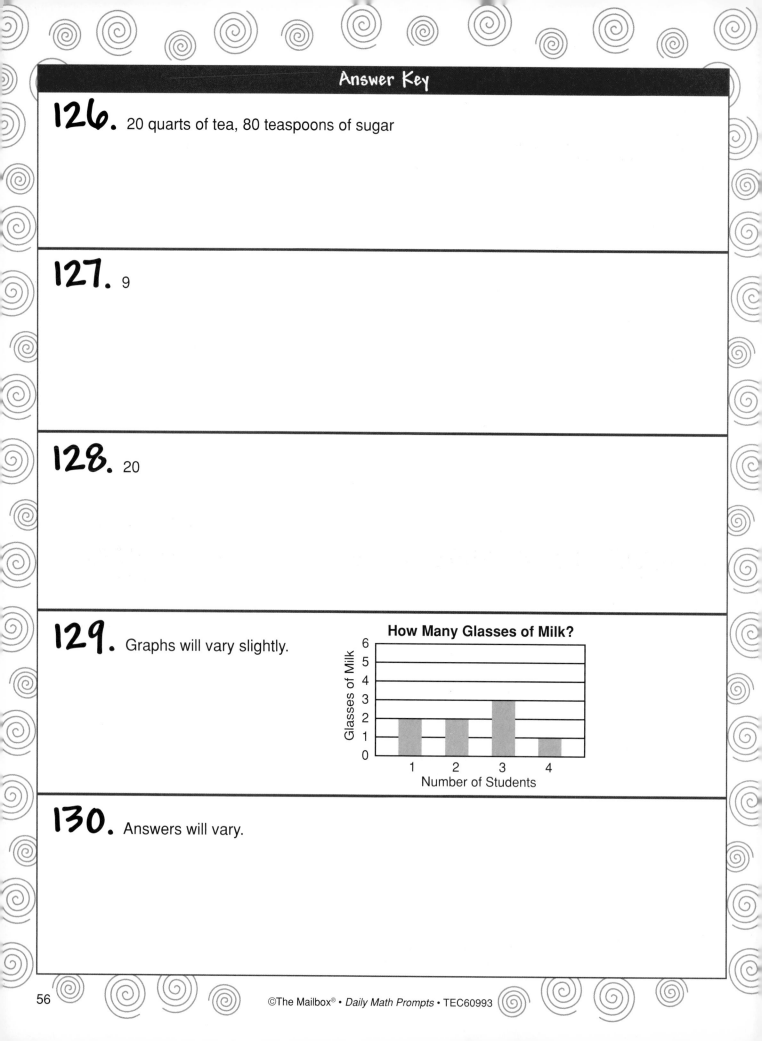

130. Answers will vary.

NUMBER & OPERATIONS

131. John is trying to guess a mystery number. The number is greater than 25 but less than 40. If you divide the number by 4, you have 3 left over. If you divide the number by 7, you have 4 left over. What is the number? How do you know?

NUMBER & OPERATIONS

132. On Monday, four friends earned $52 doing yard work. They divided the money equally among themselves. On Tuesday, each friend was paid $8 for the work he did. How much money did each friend earn in all? How do you know?

NUMBER & OPERATIONS

133. Annie has 104 apples to make pies. She is going to put 8 apples in each pie and then sell each pie for $7. If she uses all of the apples and sells all of the pies, how much money will she earn? How do you know?

GEOMETRY

134. Identify the slide, flip, and turn pattern in the row of figures shown. What will the next three figures be? How do you know?

ALGEBRA

135. What is the rule for this table? How do you know?

In	27	24	21	18	15
Out	9	8	7	6	5

131. 39

132. $21

133. $91

134.

135. Divide by 3.

NUMBER & OPERATIONS

136. If Marty has 29¢, how many possible combinations of coins does he have? How did you find your answer?

NUMBER & OPERATIONS

137. Connie has 1 five-dollar bill, 2 one-dollar bills, 1 quarter, 3 dimes, 4 nickels, and 7 pennies. A paint set costs $8.00. Does Connie have enough money to buy one? How do you know?

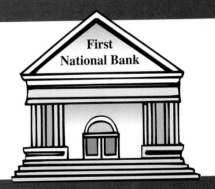

NUMBER & OPERATIONS

138. The PTA has $600 in the bank. How much is that in ten-dollar bills? How much is that in hundred-dollar bills? How do you know?

First National Bank

ALGEBRA

139. When Mary puts 3 bananas in her magic muffin machine, she gets 9 fresh muffins. When she puts in 4 bananas, she gets 12 muffins. Five bananas give her 15 muffins. What is the relationship between the number of bananas and the number of muffins? Extend the pattern to find out how many muffins Mary would get from 9 bananas. Tell how you know.

DATA ANALYSIS & PROBABILITY

140. Karen takes a fact quiz every Friday. She wants to keep track of her progress. She makes a chart like the one shown to record her scores. Do you think this will help Karen keep track of her progress? Tell why or why not.

10	20	30	40	50	60	70	80	90	100

136. 13 combinations: 1 quarter, 4 pennies; 2 dimes, 1 nickel, 4 pennies; 2 dimes, 9 pennies; 1 dime, 3 nickels, 4 pennies; 1 dime, 2 nickels, 9 pennies; 1 dime, 1 nickel, 14 pennies; 1 dime, 19 pennies; 2 nickels, 19 pennies; 5 nickels, 4 pennies; 4 nickels, 9 pennies; 3 nickels, 14 pennies; 1 nickel, 24 pennies; 29 pennies

137. no

138. 60 ten-dollar bills, 6 hundred-dollar bills

139. 27; Explanation: The machine makes three muffins for every banana Mary puts in.

140. Answers will vary.

141. Dena has $1.45 in dimes and nickels. She has 8 more nickels than dimes. How many of each coin does she have? How do you know?

142. If you have $2.47 in coins, and don't have any silver dollars or half dollars, what is the least number of coins you could have? Explain how you found your answer.

143. Keith has 3 one-dollar bills, 2 quarters, and 2 nickels. Karen has 2 one-dollar bills, 3 quarters, 3 dimes, and 1 nickel. If Keith gives Karen one of his coins, both children will have the same amount of money. Which coin could he give her so that they each have the same amount? How can you tell?

144. Imagine that you are teaching a friend how to find congruent figures. Look at the shapes. Write three questions that will help your friend find the two figures that are congruent.

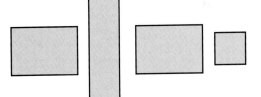

145. Curt is shopping in a bakery. There is a carrot cake that weighs 900 grams and a chocolate cake that weighs 1 kilogram. Curt wants the heavier cake, so he decides to buy the carrot cake. Is he making the right choice? Explain your answer.

141. 15 nickels, 7 dimes

142. 13 coins; 9 quarters, 2 dimes, 2 pennies

143. quarter

144. Answers will vary.

145. no

146. Barry's Bakery has 6 bags of muffins. Each bag contains 8 muffins. The bakery also has 6 boxes of cookies. Each box contains 4 cookies. How many more muffins are there than cookies? How do you know?

147. Patty says that $5.87 is the same as 5 one-dollar bills, 7 dimes, and 8 pennies. Do you agree with her? Why or why not?

148. Ronnie has $15. He wants to buy a soccer ball that costs $8.95 and a book that costs $5.60. Does he have enough money? How do you know?

149. There are 15 Ping-Pong balls in one box. How many different ways can the Ping-Pong balls be divided into two boxes? Make a table or draw pictures to show all of the possibilities.

150. Bob spins this spinner ten times. How many times do you think he lands on red? Why do you think so?

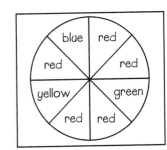

146. 24

147. no

148. yes

149. 14 different ways

Box 1	1	2	3	4	5	6	7	8	9	10	11	12	13	14
Box 2	14	13	12	11	10	9	8	7	6	5	4	3	2	1

150. Answers will vary.

NUMBER & OPERATIONS

151. Carly buys a book that costs $5.67. She pays with a ten-dollar bill. How much change should Carly get? Tell two ways that the clerk can give the change to Carly. Explain your answers.

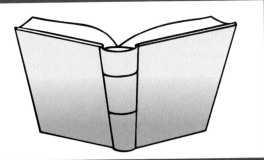

NUMBER & OPERATIONS

152. Admission to the zoo costs $7.50 for adults and $4.25 for children. How much will it cost for 3 adults and 5 children to go to the zoo? How do you know?

NUMBER & OPERATIONS

153. Stanley bought three things at the baseball game. He spent $6.55. Look at the menu. Which three things did he buy? Explain how you found your answer.

BALLPARK SNACK SHACK	
Popcorn $2.15	Hot Dog $3.25
Soda $1.75	Ice Cream $2.65
Peanuts $1.40	

MEASUREMENT

154. Grandma Bunny's rectangular garden is exactly 15 feet wide and 8 feet long. If she wants to put a fence around the garden, how much fencing should she buy? How do you know?

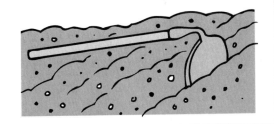

GEOMETRY

155. Sort the shapes shown into two groups. Explain your thinking.

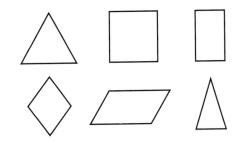

151. $4.33

152. $43.75

153. soda, popcorn, ice cream

154. 46 feet

155. Answers will vary.

156. Emily says that her egg carton is $\frac{5}{12}$ full of eggs. Look at her carton. Is she correct? Explain your answer using numbers and words.

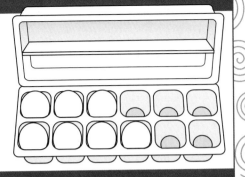

157. My denominator is three times larger than my numerator. My numerator is 2. What fraction am I?

158. Paul makes two pizzas that are the same size. He cuts one pizza into 6 equal slices. He cuts a second pizza into 8 equal slices. Which pizza has larger slices? How do you know?

159. Gary's room is 9 feet by 12 feet. He says that he needs 42 square feet of carpet. Do you agree with him? Tell why or why not.

160. Carmen is doing a probability experiment. She puts six colored cubes in a bag. Without looking, she pulls out one cube at a time, records its color, and then puts it back in the bag. When she is done, she has written the following: black, blue, blue, white, black, blue, blue, black, blue, black. How many of the cubes do you think were black? Blue? White? Explain your answer.

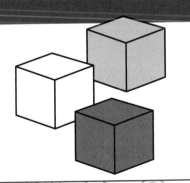

156. no

157. $\frac{2}{6}$

158. The pizza that is cut into six slices will have larger slices.

159. no; Explanation: He needs 108 square feet of carpet.

160. Answers will vary.

NUMBER & OPERATIONS

161. Sherry and Kelly each buy the same candy bar. Sherry eats $\frac{2}{3}$ of her bar. Kelly eats $\frac{4}{6}$ of her bar. Did the girls each eat the same amount of candy? Explain your answer using pictures and words.

NUMBER & OPERATIONS

162. Mark and Marie each have 16 ounces of paint. Mark uses 9 ounces of his paint. Marie uses $\frac{5}{8}$ of her paint. Who uses more paint? How do you know?

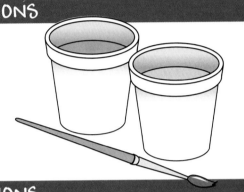

NUMBER & OPERATIONS

163. Clark bought 12 balls for the playground. Seven of them are basketballs. The rest are soccer balls. What fraction of the balls are soccer balls? How do you know?

GEOMETRY

164. Choose one of the following shapes: rectangle, square, triangle, or circle. Write a set of clues that will help a classmate guess which shape you have chosen. Read your clues again. Should you add any clues to your list? Write them now.

MEASUREMENT

165. The path is 6 yards wide and 12 yards long. What is the perimeter? What is the area? What is the difference between area and perimeter?

161. yes

162. Marie

163. $\frac{5}{12}$

164. Answers will vary.

165. 36 yards, 72 square yards

166. Nathan buys 20 apples. One-fourth of the apples are green. How many of the apples are not green? How do you know?

167. Stan grew $\frac{1}{2}$ as many flowers as Jan. Dan grew $\frac{1}{3}$ as many flowers as Stan. Jan grew 48 flowers. How many did Stan grow? How many did Dan grow? Draw a picture to help you solve the problem.

168. Ace made $\frac{4}{12}$ of the birdhouses for the spring sale. Peter made $\frac{6}{12}$ of the birdhouses. If Lee made the rest of the birdhouses, what is the fraction of the birdhouses he made? Explain how you found the answer.

169. Brian and Lynn each have 30 tennis balls. Brian has five times as many tennis balls as Keith has. Lynn has 24 more tennis balls than Keith has. How many tennis balls does Keith have? How do you know?

170. Look at the spinner below. Which one is the most fair? Explain your thinking.

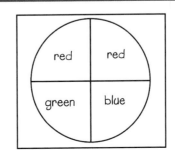
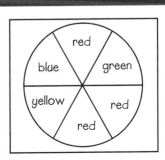

166. $\frac{3}{4}$ or 15

167. Stan grew 24; Dan grew 8.

168. $\frac{2}{12}$

169. 6

170. Answers will vary.

NUMBER & OPERATIONS

171. Aunt Polly baked 2 pies that were the same size. She cut each pie into 10 equal slices. Her family ate 1 whole pie and 6 slices of the other one. Draw a picture to show how much pie was eaten in all. Write a mixed fraction to show the total amount eaten.

NUMBER & OPERATIONS

172. Look at the numbers. Place them in order from the least to the greatest. Tell how you know.

42,867
44,046
38,791
39,254

NUMBER & OPERATIONS

173. Make a list of at least five numbers that each round down to 500. Explain your choices.

MEASUREMENT

174. Jonah's aquarium holds 10 gallons of water. If he uses a 1-quart pitcher to fill the aquarium, how many times will he have to fill the pitcher? How do you know?

GEOMETRY

175. How many total triangles are in the shape? Tell how you know.

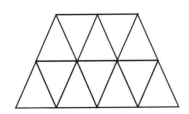

171. $1\frac{6}{10}$

172. 38,791; 39,254; 42,867; 44,046

173. Answers will vary.

174. 40.

175. 16

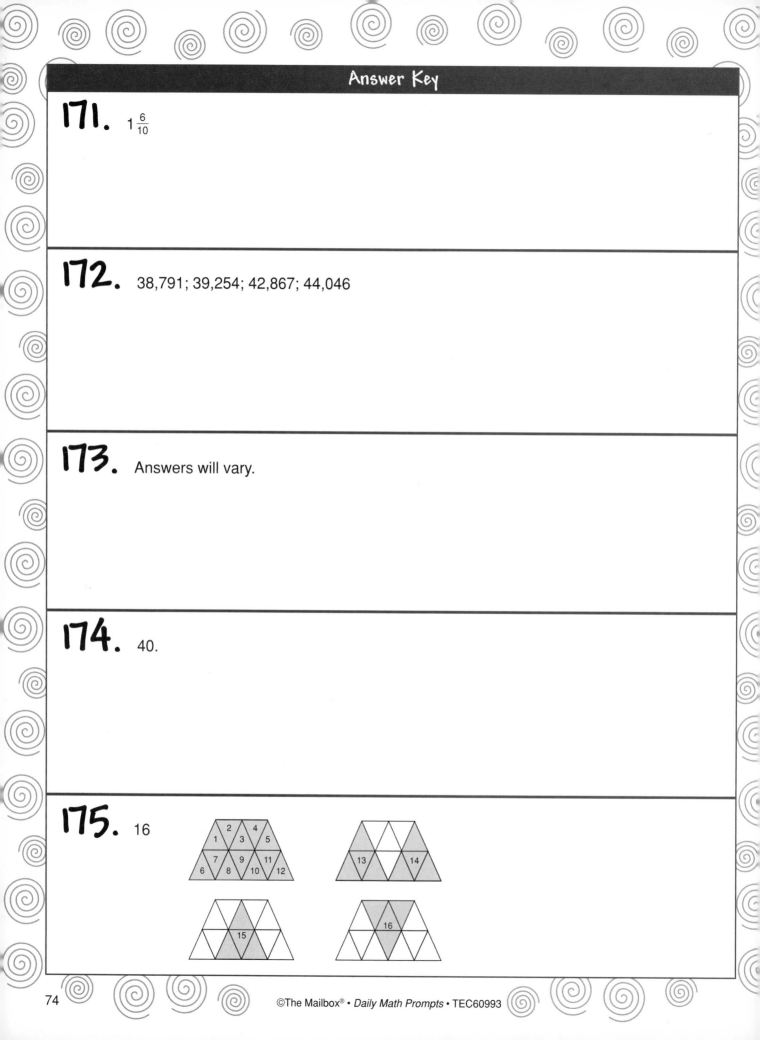

176. Ms. Thomas's class leaves for a field trip at 8:15. The bus ride takes 20 minutes. The class visits the zoo for 2 hours. Then they stop for 30 minutes to eat a snack and get ready to leave the zoo. If the ride back to school takes 20 minutes, what time does the class return to school?

177. Donna is making lunch for her friends. Sixteen of her friends want pizza. Thirteen friends want tacos. Fourteen friends want hot dogs. How many more friends want pizza than want hot dogs? How many friends are eating lunch in all? Write one more question about Donna's friends' lunches.

178. Charlie has 8 neighbors. On Monday, he makes 4 cakes for each of his neighbors. On Tuesday, he makes 1 cake for each of his neighbors. On Wednesday, he makes 3 cakes for each of his neighbors. How many cakes does he make for his neighbors in all? Explain how you know.

179. Jack has the two spinners shown. List all the possible combinations he can have if he spins both of them at the same time. Explain how you solved the problem.

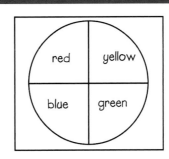 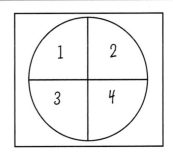

180. Sandy's marker was on (4, 4). She wanted to move it two spaces to the left. She moved it to (4, 2). Did she move the marker correctly? How do you know?

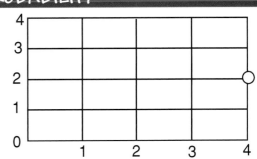

176. 11:25

177. 2, 43

178. 64

179. red, 1; red, 2; red, 3; red, 4; blue, 1;
blue, 2; blue, 3; blue, 4; green, 1;
green, 2; green, 3; green, 4; yellow, 1;
yellow, 2; yellow, 3; yellow, 4

180. no

Math Prompt Checklist

Use this handy checklist to help you keep track of each prompt used throughout the year.

✓	Prompt	✓	Prompt	✓	Prompt	✓	Prompt	✓	Prompt	✓	Prompt
	1		31		61		91		121		151
	2		32		62		92		122		152
	3		33		63		93		123		153
	4		34		64		94		124		154
	5		35		65		95		125		155
	6		36		66		96		126		156
	7		37		67		97		127		157
	8		38		68		98		128		158
	9		39		69		99		129		159
	10		40		70		100		130		160
	11		41		71		101		131		161
	12		42		72		102		132		162
	13		43		73		103		133		163
	14		44		74		104		134		164
	15		45		75		105		135		165
	16		46		76		106		136		166
	17		47		77		107		137		167
	18		48		78		108		138		168
	19		49		79		109		139		169
	20		50		80		110		140		170
	21		51		81		111		141		171
	22		52		82		112		142		172
	23		53		83		113		143		173
	24		54		84		114		144		174
	25		55		85		115		145		175
	26		56		86		116		146		176
	27		57		87		117		147		177
	28		58		88		118		148		178
	29		59		89		119		149		179
	30		60		90		120		150		180

Assessment Rubric

Student: _____

Prompt #: _____ Date: _____

Answer:

☐ **2** Answered correctly
☐ **1** Partial answer given; copied wrong problem; computation error
☐ **0** Answered incorrectly; no answer given

Understanding:

☐ **2** Understands fully the math needed
☐ **1** Understands most of the math needed
☐ **0** Understands little of the math needed

Comments: _____
_____

Explanation:

☐ **2** Communicated ideas clearly
☐ **1** Communicated ideas fairly well
☐ **0** Communicated ideas poorly

Comments: _____
_____

Score = ☐

Assessment Rubric

Student: _____

Prompt #: _____ Date: _____

Answer:

☐ **2** Answered correctly
☐ **1** Partial answer given; copied wrong problem; computation error
☐ **0** Answered incorrectly; no answer given

Understanding:

☐ **2** Understands fully the math needed
☐ **1** Understands most of the math needed
☐ **0** Understands little of the math needed

Comments: _____
_____

Explanation:

☐ **2** Communicated ideas clearly
☐ **1** Communicated ideas fairly well
☐ **0** Communicated ideas poorly

Comments: _____
_____

Score = ☐

_____'s

Journal

$$4 \times 2 = 8$$

Prompt Number: _____   Date: _____

Prompt Number: _____   Date: _____